GROWING UP
IN SIMPLER TIMES ...
MEMORIES OF
LINCOLN PARK

Boyhood Memories Brought To Life

Donald Walter Wallace

DEDICATION

This book is dedicated to the people of Lincoln Park, whose parents and grandparents during the 1930's and 40's were part of America's greatest generation, who suffered but survived the long hard years of the great depression and the years of World War II as well. These are my true memories of growing up during those years in Lincoln Park, MI. I hope you enjoy my stories which are as real and alive in my memory today as they were the day they happened and that they bring back memories of simpler times for you.

—Donald Walter Wallace

March 2013, Loudon, TN

TABLE OF CONTENTS

My parents, Walter and Julia Wallace,
wedding picture, 1927, Detroit, MI

My sister Norma's 1ˢᵗ Communion, age 9,
and myself age 3, Detroit, MI 1935

I

VAST OPEN FIELDS, DIRT AND GRAVEL ROADS...

Lincoln Park at first sight 75 years ago....Riding with my mother on my first bus ride to Lincoln Park in the summer of 1937 is still in my thoughts to this day. The trip from Detroit to look at our new home still under construction, but not ready to move in yet.... We left the bus at Fort and Champaign walking toward the new high school, stopping mid-block at a small red brick restaurant, my mother ordering a hamburger for each of us and a cold bottle of pop to eat outside under a large shade tree in front of the little diner (which I learned later was owned by the Martin family who shared living quarters in the rear who many years later owned a party store at Dix and Pagel). While walking to McLain Street I remember being in awe of the massive three story building and the Lincoln Park high school that I in later years would spend many happy years playing football on Sunday afternoons on the front lawn. I recall swinging on the flag pole chain almost to Lafayette Street and back then letting go before hitting the steel flag pole with our little bodies. The memories of the vast open fields and dirt and gravel roads, a wooden house here and there are unlike what I remembered in Detroit

1

and the two family upper flat that I was born at. Moving in and living the first year without electricity, but with oil lanterns and an oil stove in the middle of the living room.... To this day when I have occasion to drive past the little red brick building in mid-block on Champaign Street, can't help but remember sitting under the now gone shade tree with my mother, munching on a hamburger and sharing a single bottle of pop some 75 years ago, and perhaps a smile thinking of the memories of so long ago.

II

FIRST DAY OF SCHOOL.... LETTING GO OF MY MOM'S HAND....

First day in school....Memories from the late 1930s, walking hand in hand with my mother approaching the huge red brick building on Champaign and Fort, with fear as to what lay ahead in this big scary building.... My mother recalled to me some years ago that she dressed me in a new white shirt and tie, knickers and long stockings (the style of the day) with almost new shoes. Entering a large noisy room filled with other little kids, some crying and the rest as I, just looking wide eyed about the room. Now it was time for the mothers to leave with a promise that she would return soon for the walk home.... The sounds of kids crying increased as the classroom door was closed by an unknown lady who we were later told was a teacher. All of us were seated on the wooden floor of the room frightened with wide eyes until my mother returned. Living a couple of blocks from Goodell school, with mostly open fields and high weeds, I don't recall my mother walking me to school any more after the first day, but am sure she would have. So the days and weeks passed, recalling that all of the kids would walk home for lunch and return by themselves. I loved school during those early days, making new friends, some that would last a lifetime, and walking together back and forth to the neighborhood with only mostly the birds and a few cars passing to break the silence of the times.

III

THE "WPA"
WORK PROJECTS
ADMINISTRATION

During the long mid depression years of 1939, the government introduced a newly formed work program to the country called the "WPA" or the "Works Progress Administration". It was the original government stimulus as we know it today. The government plan was to put millions of people back to work building roads, sidewalks, parks, bridges, etc. across the country. Unemployment in 1939 was at 19 percent among whites and 50 percent for blacks in the inner cities. I remember as a six year old boy in Lincoln Park, the WPA came to our gravel street "McLain" in 1939. Standing on the sidewalk in awe of dozens and dozens of men whom appeared with long handled shovels and picks, to begin digging by hand an underground sewer line on our side of the street..... I have no memory of any kind of earth moving machines being brought in, just dozens of men swinging a pick or digging with shovels, with the silence of the times, all you could hear was the sounds of shovels and picks hitting the ground, and a few grunts as the sewer line became deeper and deeper.... I recall that many of the workers were wearing white dress shirts, some with ties, and all with hats, the "style" of the 1930s. I remember a little man the workers called "Shorty", he was the water carrier for the job, with a pail of cool water and a long handled ladle, he would walk back and forth among the men in the hot sun. A call out to "Shorty" brought a cool drink from the same pail and ladle that was used by dozens of other men earlier.... It reminded me of a chain gang movie, with the men sweating in the hot sun and being given cool water from the same pail. I still wonder today, how many of the men digging in the trench may have been office workers, lawyers or farmers, just happy to have a job to be able to feed his family. Old sidewalks in Lincoln Park, if still found, will show WPA stamped into the cement, perhaps by our fathers or grandfathers during the years of the great depression and very hard times for all people in Lincoln Park and the country over 70 years ago.

IV

WALKING PAST A
CLIMBABLE TREE WAS
UNHEARD OF....

To an eight or nine year old boy during the 1930s, the thought of walking past a climbable tree was unheard of, as the bigger and taller trees seemed to attract us kids the most. The field where the Lincoln Park High School now stands had some of the best trees along the creek and railroad and it was all there for us kids to claim on any warm summer day. Floating around barefoot on a raft or sitting next to the camp fire roasting potatoes from a neighbor's garden.... The quiet of the days, only broken by the sound of a car or truck bumping over the railroad crossing on Champaign Street, the distant barking of a dog or the croaking of the little frogs in the wet fields.... My leather high tops and long stockings under my corduroy knickers were always best for climbing trees due to the heavy bark that would cut your legs as you slid down to the ground. Climbing up...up...up...without thinking to look down, only made it worst as you reached a dizzy height of 10 to 15 feet or higher, then the sudden fear of climbing and sliding back down holding onto the tree for dear life until feeling the ground on your feet.... A vivid memory of climbing a tall tree on Mill Street at the railroad tracks, to a height where you could look north and see the smoking chimneys of the Ford factory, the thought of coming back down and sudden fear, vowing never to climb that high again.... With dirty faces and hands from the tree bark and blackened potato skins that we had cooked on our open fire, it was time to head home. My mother could always tell by the condition of my corduroy knickers that I was in the trees again, so with a very stern warning she warned me to never climb trees again with my school knickers "or else"! "Or else" from my mother was something you never wanted to hear again. So a few days later with my two friends it was back to our creek, where they began climbing again, and with my mother's voice still in my head, I took off my high tops and floated about on our raft in bare feet keeping it all to myself, while looking up at Eric and Bert climbing higher and higher, probably to a height of 15 feet, but who cared, I knew my mother would check my knickers when I got home only to find them wet from the creek. I felt good that I kept my word to her about climbing....until next week....! I wonder how many kids today have ever climbed a tree to the dizzy height of 15 feet or more in their school pants? If not, they have missed out on some of the best times for little boys and girls, never mind the baking of potatoes near the creek and the railroad, or the picking of wild raspberries as far as the eye could see....

V

ELECTION DAY FOR AN LITHUANIAN FAMILY IN THE 1930'S

Election Day brings back memories going back to the late thirties and as a little boy getting ready to go with my parents to vote in the presidential election. My father came to this country from Lithuania in 1913, and some years later became a U.S. citizen. I still remember seeing the pride on his face when he talked about his citizenship in America even many years later. It was voting day in those early days in Lincoln Park.... Both of my parents would dress in their best clothing, my dad in his only brown suit and mom in her best dress..... The three of us walked to the Goodell School to vote on this important day. In those old days, the city would bring in a little wooden, dark green building that was called a voting booth, and set up on the Fort Park side of the school. From a short distance I could see the smoke coming from the small smoke stack on the roof of the voting booth. I don't remember if a line was present, but probably not. I entered the little dark green voting booth with my parents noticing a small cast iron coal stove on the old wood plank floor almost glowing red from the fire inside. The voting attendant furnished my parents with a dark pencil and a sheet of paper where they marked their vote......and that was it. I kind of hated to leave the warmth of the little wooden building for the walk home to McLain Street. My mother told me years later that voting day in Lincoln Park was the most important day for him, all dressed up in his only suit, because he was now a American citizen and just full of pride on this special day. How times have changed, now with computer voting, long lines, hanging tabs etc. I think that some people who wait in long lines would envy us in the old days getting dressed up in our best and walking through the smoky little dark green wooden building that was my parents voting booth at Goodell school. My father's pride spilled over on that day because he was finally a real American citizen....

Playing with my dog on the front lawn of our house, McClain Street, Lincoln Park, MI 1938

VI

A LITTLE LITHUANIAN VEGETARIAN DOG...

As a little boy growing up in Lincoln Park during the early 1940s, I am sure the more I think about it, that I must have had the only little Lithuanian dog that was vegetarian in the city. Lithuanian because my dad coming from the old country, gave our dog a Lithuanian name that was hard for me to pronounce, and vegetarian because I trained him that way. Our dinner table had vegetables piled high almost every night, due to my dad's garden. They were called "Victory Gardens" in the war years, so as most young kids, vegetables were not our food of choice, but because they were cooked, you would be forced to enjoy them, or else... With my little dog sitting under the table at my feet, as dad would turn away from the table even for a second, he would be given a hand full of the goodies from my plate. He learned to love them almost as much as I loved getting them off my plate in a hurry, so I could get back outside with my friends. My dear old dad never learned that his vegetables were being turned into dog food! I lived a charmed childhood I guess, but that little Lithuanian dog whose name I could never pronounce (i.e. "Pupsee"), lived a long and happy life, maybe due to the fact I turned him into a vegetarian from dad's victory garden....Sorry Pop....RIP....

VII

The Aroma of Mrs. Cooper's Bread....

Neighborhood memories from 1939, the quiet warm summer days in the late 1930's, meant that the house windows and doors would be open for all to enjoy the scent of the then clear air in Lincoln Park. But above even the clean air, was the not to be forgotten was the aroma of freshly baked bread from the home of Mrs. Cooper in the 1400 block of McLain Street. The kids at the Cooper house were the first family I met in the early days, and Bob Cooper was in my kindergarten class at Goodell School. Bob's mother made the most delicious freshly baked bread, and if the breeze was right we in the next block would get the full effect of the aroma through our open windows. I remember my mother would go to our side garden and fill a bag with fresh tomatoes and green beans to be taken to Mrs. Cooper in exchange for a loaf of her still warm bread.... Quickly walking with my wagon of produce, Mrs. Cooper would yell through the screen door to come in with my bag of garden fresh tomatoes where she would then wrap the warm bread in a kitchen towel for me to carry home. Can't forget holding the bread in my arm to enjoy the aroma, knowing when I got home my mother would quickly slice a couple of pieces putting a small amount of farm butter on each piece, so now the aroma of the bread would fill our little kitchen for a short time until my dad got home from work. A couple of days would pass and again the aroma of Mrs. Cooper's wonderful homemade bread would fill the little neighborhood. At times she would send a loaf of warm bread with her little daughter to be given to my mother. In those days that is what good neighbors did for each other, and when more green beans were ready, back into the paper bag and I would run to the Cooper house, without knocking and handing the bag to a beaming, thankful, good neighbor....

VII

NEISNER FIVE
AND DIME....

I remember my mother and me walking hand in hand to downtown Lincoln Park for shopping with her black leather shopping bag tucked under her arm to later be filled with groceries. Crossing Southfield at Fort Street, Woolworths was always the first stop, walking inside on the old wooden floors that creaked at times, the wonderful smell of those old dry goods stores stays with me still today. The sales ladies all wearing colorful aprons and many with their pencil tucked into their hair bun. Mom always bought new thread for sewing, as I stood on my tip toes gazing at the many sales counters that were mostly filled with things I had never seen before. I recall that the sidewalks would be busy with people walking with shopping bags filled. The newspaper man on the corner of Fort & Southfield would have his papers stacked high, waiting for the cars that would line the curb in front of Woolworths for the weekend paper to be carried to their car window. Almost all of the stores had the old type crank out sun awnings in front, while the hand crank was always left in place for the rollup at the end of the day. Neisner Five and Dime was my favorite dry goods store. I remember passing the free weight scale on the sidewalk in front, and my mother always giving me a coin to be put in the cloth cap of the poor man without legs selling pencils for a living in front of Neiser's. I'd walk inside Neisner Five and Dime, with my mother warning me not stare over my shoulder at the poor man, but I always managed to do so out of the corner of my eyes. Mom would let me walk away from her so I could run to the large toy counter, overflowing with cars, trucks and everything a little boy would dream of. My gaze was on a beautiful Hopalong Cassidy Cap Gun and Holster set hanging overhead, my mother took out her small change purse after watching me gaze of this wonderful gun set. No need to put it in a bag, I strapped on this two gun set at the counter, my mother knowing I could have not wanted anything more than this. Strutting out of Neisner Five and Dime, now with the real Hopalong Cassady Holster with two guns strapped around me, I walked down the sidewalk hoping I would be seen by other kids, but don't know if anyone noticed. A stop at the Old Maids Hamburger Place, a little 8 to 10 stool place, for a five cent burger and a pop was always treat. Sometimes we would go into the Park Sweet Shop run by Mary for a fresh baked pastry that would be taken out of the front window display. Great memories of simple times in downtown Lincoln Park!

IX

MY FIRST JOB AT
URBAN'S & THE GREAT
BANANA HEIST

More memories of my favorite Lincoln Park Mom and Pop grocery stores from the 1930's and 1940's.... John Urban's grocery store at Fort Park and Champaign, was the first little neighborhood store we shopped at during 1937 when we moved to Lincoln Park. Recall that Mr. Urban and his wife were the sole employees at that time, I was later a "stock and delivery boy". The family lived upstairs and Mrs. Urban's home cooked meals were ever present the minute you came through the front door, sounding the little bell most little stores had during those times. There was the little white meat counter at the rear of the store with sawdust on the floor, Mr. Urban slicing a few pieces of lunch meat for your order, then wrapping it in white butcher paper and string from the spool hanging from above the counter....The tinkling of the doorbell meant another customer for Mrs. Urban at the front door register, always in an old but clean flowered apron, the kind my mother had. Cash money was not necessary during those early depression years, your sale was written in "The Book" where later in the month you came in and made a payment on your account, as all customers were from the neighborhood. Business appeared to always be good, from the kids with their pennies from the Goodell School across the street, to the high school kids walking past after school. At eight years old Mr. Urban hired me as a stock and delivery boy, so with my wagon, I would deliver some of the orders for the neighbors, but never had to collect money, as everything was put on "The Book". I never will forget sweeping the basement one day. A large stock of bananas were hanging from the rafter to ripen, temptation overcame me, all those beautiful bananas just hanging there in front of my eyes. Mom could never afford them at home, so standing on a box I took a single banana, and with my heart pounding and watching the basement steps in fear that Mr. Urban would come down. I gulped down that wonderful tasting little banana and hid the peeling in the overhead wooden rafter. I got to thinking what my dad would do to me if he knew what I just did, but the Lord was with this little eight year old boy that day, so I worked a few more weeks until school started, and left my first job with guilt in my heart. I still wonder some seventy five years later, if that little peel from the best banana I ever enjoyed is still hidden in the basement rafters of that little Mom and Pop grocery store....

X

THE SOUNDS OF SILENCE

Living in a small unfinished house across the field from the high school, with no more than three houses on my block, large open fields for a little boy to explore, and the constant sound of silence. Listening to birds in the distance, an occasional car on Champaign St. or the distant sound of the 5:30 pm passenger train as it became nearer to Lincoln Park and then passing Champaign St. with a roar, then out of sight and the sound of silence again. In 1939, I would go door to door with my wagon full of fresh produce from our garden, selling it for small change. Monday morning was a day that most women did their washing, the sight of the white sheets in the rear yards blowing in the breeze reminded me of sails on ships that we saw in the movies. This being in the midst of the depression, most clothing showed signs of the tough times we were living in. Fresh baked bread and pastries from the Mill's bakery truck delivered to your home with the milk coming daily, and after calling out his name, he delivered your milk in glass bottles right into your kitchen and to the ice box. Summer days were spent going to the woods game hunting, leaving your home early in the morning with the pockets of your corduroy knickers stuffed with potatoes for

21

roasting. My two little friends were also dressed in corduroy knickers and high tops with a small knife in the boot pocket. Two of us were armed with little Daisy BB guns, except for little Bert who only carried a bow without arrows. Our hunting area was where the present high school and I-75 now stand, but then it was filled with woods and large open fields. Anyone who has ever owned corduroy pants knows the "swishing" sound they make when you walk. Well, the three of us hunters were all wearing old corduroy knickers with long stockings, and I am sure this alerted the big game of our approach, so lucky for them, our hunt ended without a single BB leaving our guns. Finally to the creek that was alongside the railroad tracks and our old wooden door we used to float on in knee deep creek water, after taking off our leather high tops. Roasting the potatoes in the hot coals until burnt black, then feasting on our hot dinner, faces black from the burnt potato skins and stained red from the wild Raspberries found along the tracks. The distant whistle of the 5:30 Red Arrow Passenger Train began our hearts pounding as the monster approached at high speed, fear set in as we were to blame if the monster suddenly derailed after running over a penny we put on the rail. Flying past the three little boys wide eyed, and hands cupping our ears, the engineer waived to his little audience, as he always did, and disappeared from view, and again the sound of silence. Time to head home after a fun day in our hunting grounds, where we were sure our mothers would make us take a bath after looking at our faces. Tomorrow was another day….maybe back to the forest or the creek for rafting or just listening to the sound of silence….

XI

LINCOLN PARK DAYS AT BOB-LO ISLAND

Lincoln Park days and Bob-Lo Island….The little city of Lincoln Park during the 1940's, proclaimed "Lincoln Park Day" as a city holiday by the Mayor and City Council….a day to be spent at Bob-Lo Island for a day of fun for all. Weeks prior to the holiday, most businesses would display colorful window signs of the date and place of the one day holiday….Most city businesses would close as well as the city's only bank at Fort and O'Connor. On the day of the city holiday, my two friends and I, escorted by my friend's mother, would pack and carry a lunch in a shoe box tied with a string. Early on the warm morning we began the long walk from our homes in the high school neighborhood, to Emmons, then to Bishop Park in Wyandotte. The first sight of the huge Bob-Lo boat began our hearts pounding with excitement of the day to come. The long lines were already forming at the boat dock when the boat horn sounded and we began pushing forward to board the huge boat, always careful not to drop our shoe box with our day's lunch. Leaving Wyandotte for the cruise meant kids running all over the moving boat, up the stairs to the top deck then back down the crowded stairs stopping to look at the visible engine room in motion. Arriving at the Bob-Lo dock, the mad dash of little kids under the covered dock-way to find a picnic table under a shade tree for my friend's mother and our box lunches and when we did, it was off running and laughing from one ride to the next. This was something we kids had never even dreamed about, let alone be free to run and have this kind of fun....The Mayor and City Council members that were present would have foot races while inside a burlap potato sack, horse shoe pitching, softball games and all to the sound of music and dancing coming from the large covered pavilion....Then all too soon, it was time to leave after the sounding of the steam horn of our boat, meaning our day of new adventure was almost over. We walked slowly back on the covered dock to the waiting boat that would return us back to Bishop park where it all began. The cruise back was quiet compared to the early ride of the morning, as most of the wooden folding chairs were now taken by tired parents and their kids. Finally docking in Wyandotte, and then began the long walk home to Lincoln Park carrying our empty shoe boxes, and talking of next year and another " Lincoln Park day " then hearing the sound in the distance of the Bob-Lo boat horn, only meant another fun day for kids and family's on their way to Bob-Lo island.

XII

THE SATURDAY 12 CENT MATINEE...

For only 12 cents, the highlight for a young boy on almost any winter weekend during the early days of WWII was to stand on a sidewalk in the cold, with your wool hat pulled down almost over your eyes, nose running, with a hundred other yelling and pushing rowdy young kids most all wearing the same type wool hat waiting while the line is growing around the corner of the Lincoln Park Theatre....my older sister guarding the quarter mom gave us to spend as we wished. While I held tightly to my Holloway sucker, bedlam began as the long line began to move slowly again, more yelling and pushing as we finally entered the big dark theatre, running and pushing to sit in the very first row, with the crescendo of noise now at a roar, finally seated and almost looking straight up, the music began, first with ten cartoons, a Roy Rogers cowboy picture and then John Wayne as a fighter pilot blasting "Japs" out of the air. Loud cheers with each and even louder boos when our hero kissed a girl. After what seemed like hours and a sore neck from the effects of the first row, the theatre was lighted, another mad dash to leave ahead of the next group of rowdy little kids. Heaven forbid if you lost your wool hat in the dark room. Once outside your mind went to the next weekend and another sore neck. Wow! All of this for a twelve cent ticket! What ever happened to my youth in that magic building known then as the Lincoln Park Theater in 1942?

XIII

THE FUN HOUSE...THE
LINCOLN PARK THEATRE

You really had to be there during the early 1940's, to recall the mayhem and excitement of spending an entire Saturday afternoon, and for some part of the evening as well….at the Lincoln Park show with a couple of hundred screaming kids my age. This was never to be forgotten! For the grand sum of twelve cents, you could spend almost endless hours in this fun house for kids, finally away from Mother and freedom many for the first time. With the lights dimming and screen music beginning, it finally was what we all waited all week for......cartoons and more cartoons to satisfy the little audience, now all jumping up and down to the words when the weekly serials would be flashed on the screen. Pulse pounding thrills, spills and chills as "Smiling Jack" and his men or "Gangbusters" machine guns blazing, "Tarzan and the Apes", "Jungle Girl" or "Tailspin Tommy" always brought more screaming….Then the tough "Dead End Kids" to settle the crowd down for a bit, and the favorite of all…."The Three Stooges" almost caused some little ones to put their fingers in their ears due to the yelling and laughing. Maybe a "Tom Mix" or "Red Rider" with almost the smell of gunpowder filling the little room from endless gun fights, and the loud boos when Gene Autry began to sing while on his horse, or when he kissed the school teacher....Next week it would be "Hopalong Cassidy". After three or more hours of this, you began to see mothers walking up and down the darkened isles calling out their kids names to come home. How embarrassing it was to have your mother standing at your aisle, while the other kids who may have stayed until they began sweeping the floor, laughed as your mother took you by the hand in front of the whole world and walked you out. Good Grief Ma! Only six more days to another Saturday afternoon in the fun house for the little kids of Lincoln Park....

XIV

A TOUCH OF MAYBERRY IN LINCOLN PARK

A touch of Mayberry in Lincoln Park....Memories of my favorite "Mom & Pop" grocery store of the 1940's....The pleasant aroma of dinner cooking could not escape you as you pass the screen door, on a busy Fort Street sidewalk on any given summer day during the 1940's and later....The tinkle of the small bell and the slamming of the spring held screen door as you entered the small store was not to be forgotten by passing time. The dinner cooking in the rear living quarters, and the aroma, made the visit something to look forward to this young boy. Walking over the old creaking wooden floors, and the movement of the hanging fly strips moving in rhythm to the overhead ceiling fan, small freshly painted signs covering the front windows telling of the daily sales, it was an old fashioned grocery store of its era. The side wall lined with wooden shelving filled with canned and boxed goods, only to be reached by the long handled gripping claw, a must in its day.... Behind the center meat counter, a dapper man in a long white butcher's apron, wrapping a meat purchase in white butcher paper from the roll attached to the counter.... Another tinkle of the bell and the slamming of the screen door meant another customer to serve. My usual purchase of a Faygo cream soda, was a real treat to this little boy. My nickel or dime spent here always earned me a smile and a thank you from the man or his wife, always to be remembered to this day. A little touch of "Mayberry" in Lincoln Park long ago.... Many years later, I recall driving past this same little grocery store on Fort Street during the summer evenings, observing the friendly man and his wife seated on old wooden kitchen chairs on the front sidewalk, waiving to friends and passersby. Michael "Mickey" Karol, a proud man, could always be recognized walking down Fort Street, dressed in his finest suit, white shoes and straw hat, always with his trademark of a long cigarette holder, and always a wave. Definitely, in my opinion, a Lincoln Park institution and pioneer family of days long passed, always quick to smile and say thank you to a little boy spending a nickel or dime in his little grocery store. Karol's grocery, east side of Fort Street between Lincoln and Garfield, will always be my favorite "mom & pop" grocery store to be remembered! What was your favorite little "mom & pop" store from the past?

XV

OUR "BUNK"

Lincoln Park 75 years ago was a vast area of open fields and narrow gravel roads in the neighborhoods mostly south of Southfield Road, blocks without a house but open fields for little boys to explore and claim as their own, little traffic and the stillness of the summer days with only the sounds of Bob White quails calling breaking the silence of the morning. Summer mornings at my house started with my two little friends, Eric and Bert, calling my name under my bedroom window, usually by 7:30 am. So with a cold glass of Ovaltine to drink, I was out the back door after telling my mother I would be home for supper. Imagine! So it was out to explore a new day with my friends and dog. What to do today? Head to our creek at the railroad to float about on our old wooden door we called our raft, or spend the day at out private little palace away from mom's eyes, that we called our "bunk" in an open field across from the Lincoln Park High School.... To a little boy our "bunk" meant freedom for the day to do as we wished. A bunker or "bunk" was nothing more than two holes we dug into the clay, just big enough for us to sit in and crawl on our hands and knees, with a roof of cardboard and old boards, and a passageway dug from one small room to the next. To sit on the ground with your two little friends was our first taste of freedom, to the first time taking a puff on a Corn Cobb Pipe with pipe tobacco from Eric's dad's desk.... So with my pocket stuffed with mom's kitchen matches that came from over the stove, and a couple of potatoes to bake in the ground, and my dad's shovel on my shoulder, we crossed the open field to our private place in the warm ground. Passing the many planted victory gardens in the vacant fields, we helped ourselves to fresh produce to be stored in our "bunk" for later times including green apples.... Pulling away the cardboard door cover, we slipped into the little room and began building a small fire of twigs on the dirt floor, a little fire was always a must, so with the twigs beginning to burn, the task of getting rid of the smoke was never on our minds, until the little dirt room filled with smoke. With no place to go, we began climbing over each other to push the cardboard away from the entrance and we climbed out into the fresh air with tears in our eyes. We pulled away the old roof boards to exit the smoke.... Then it was back into the bunk for a snack of a chocolate cup cake from Eric's mothers bread box and passing a single bottle of warm Faygo orange from one mouth to the next, being careful to only take "one swig at a time". Sitting back looking up at the warm blue sky, we knew that our little palace was all we needed in our young lives. So with the tomatoes and cucumbers eaten, it was almost time to leave our private little bunk for home and supper. It was the end to an almost full day, my mother meeting me at the back door telling me to take off my dirty knickers and long socks for washing on the board, I sat down to supper with my dad and sister in my underwear.... But tomorrow was a new warm summer day to head for our private creek at the railroad to just float around on the old door, to catch a frog maybe, or to roast our potatoes in the fire pit, waiting for the 5:30 pm passenger steam train at Champaign to come roaring down the tracks going south, and waiving at the engineer with his goggles and red bandanna around his neck, who never failed to waive back at the three little barefoot boys wide eyed with their hands over their ears. Then in a second it had passed and it was nothing more than a small dot getting smaller and smaller as it headed down the rails and then disappeared.... So now again, in almost total silence as we headed home for supper with shoes in hand....tomorrow was another new day to explore the vast open world of Lincoln Park to three kids and my dog, but with clean knickers and high socks.

XVI

THE DEPRESSION YEARS...
HARD TIMES FOR ALL

Our parents lived with hard times daily with no jobs and very little money, but most were a tough bunch in those days. As I think back, the mothers in our little neighborhood on McLain Street were much the same….hard working and can't recall my own mother except on Sunday when it was time for the long walk to St. Henrys church and mass, that she was not wearing her apron over her simple flowered cotton dress, as did most of the others in Lincoln Park. The apron was worn to the grocery store under their coats and everywhere else. I can hardly remember a time that as a little boy going to Goodell school not wearing anything but darned socks over and over and little patches at times when needed over your Knickers…. Never felt anything about this as most kids were wearing hand me downs usually too large. Most of the kids had their hair cut at home, no hiding this, even little girls as I recall…. Vivid memories of sitting on the old, frayed living room rug that was given to us by friends, watching my mother darning a pile of socks using the wooden spindle, and my dad with his one good ear almost pressed against the little table radio, listening to the news of the dark days forming in Europe and world war to come.... Recall my dad fixing my leather shoes in the basement with the iron form that he would place my shoe on upside down, and nail on the used leather soles that were pieces of old conveyor belts brought home from the automotive plant where my dad worked, as they were discarded, then trimmed with a knife around the edges. So from patched Knickers to socks were darned over and over to the old leather soles on your shoes, it was off to Goodell school with your friends who at times had more different colored patches than yourself. Lincoln Park families all, and with memories that are still with me. And many years before unemployment compensation to families, but a small welfare food item, a block of cheese, was available....Without a victory garden in your side yard, many families would do without this luxury food....

XVII

GAMES KIDS PLAYED

Mumbly Peg was played a lot with a knife….can't recall any of us kids getting cut and guess we were just lucky. In today's world, if a parent knew that their kids were playing this game with knives, they would be arrested for sure! "Duck on the Rock" a favorite game of ours during the 1940's, played with old pet milk cans were the best. In the middle of Champaign Street we would draw a circle, and the first kid put his can on top of the rock in the middle of the circle while the other kids outside the circle would throw their can trying to knock the can off the rock before he was tagged. We almost had the street to ourselves due to lack of traffic most of the time. Again with Pet milk cans and with our leather soled shoes, we would stomp on the can until it was attached to your shoe, then do the other one. Imagine the racket that was made by a bunch of kids running on the sidewalk with cans on the bottom of your shoes, we called this horseshoes....

XVIII

DUG OUT BASEMENTS AND MUD BALL WARS

Remember when the old steam shovels would began digging basements for new homes? In the McLain and Mill Street neighborhood, we little kids could not wait to have "Mud Ball Wars" against each other, from one hill of clay to the other. To get hit by a hard mud ball was not to be forgotten, but the next day we would do it all over again. Must have been a Lincoln Park thing! We would play tag in newly built houses, climbing on the roof rafters and never falling….and us eight or nine year olds - after basement walls were installed around the hole, they would place the steel I-beam main support from the front to the back of the block walls - we would take turns walking the I-beam which was about eight inches across. Once you got in the middle of the beam, some of the boys would began throwing mud balls at you until you got to the end of the wall…. Fall we did, into the dirt floor of the newly dug basement, which was about eight to ten feet high. We came home many a night with black and blue marks on our bodies from our little "friends" finding their mark with a hard bud ball. I sometimes wonder how I made it past 10 years old in those "fun" days growing up in Lincoln Park during the early 1940's, from climbing on moving railroad box cars, to mud balls, and once in a while falling out of a tree….Thank you Lord!

XIX

HOWARD THE FLOWER MAN

He was only known by the shoppers and business people in downtown Lincoln Park during the early forties as "Howard the Flower Man". I remember him as a gentle soul of a man who was obviously mentally handicapped from birth, living with his parents in a little house on the back of the lot on McLain Street which was almost hidden from view from the high bushes that surrounded the entire little house. To us little kids from down the street he was just "Howard", never knowing his last name, but to a bunch of little kids it really didn't matter.... During the summer months, Howard would be seen coming from the yard of his house with his little wagon filled with assorted flowers that his mother placed in the wagon, and he began his slow walk down Fort Park to downtown Lincoln Park. I recall that he would stop in front of Neisse's Five and Dime, waiting for his customers, shoppers and business men and woman who all knew the gentle little man who I never remember saying anything but the word "Hi" in his gentle voice to anyone. We all knew Howard as a special friend who was different than other people like us, even to little kids he was greeted with respect and friendship....little kids could be so cruel at times, but when it came to Howard he was our friend and he was treated by all in that kindly manner. To this day I can still picture "Howard the Flower Man" pulling his mostly empty wagon back down Fort Park to the little house on McLain Street only to return a day or two later to greet his customers in downtown Lincoln Park with a few more home grown flowers that only produced small change I am sure, due to the depression days, but still he was given something for his labor and friendly smile. But only uttering the word "Hi" was enough to the kind people of Lincoln Park who many were without, to feel in their hearts that they in a small way they made life more pleasant to the gentle little man known as Howard the Flower Man....

It seemed that Howard was with us for so many of our young years, then suddenly, the little man and his wagon was not to be seen any more like he just faded away. As I look back now, my wish is that I would have gone to that little house on McLain Street and perhaps spoken to his mother, but that was not to be.... A new modern home now sits where Howard and his mother lived, strange, but I still think of Howard from time to time and some seventy years later. I am sure that God gives us these beautiful special people for a purpose, to give joy to so many others in his own way, and am sure that his heart was filled with pleasure as he pulled his little wagon filled with his mother's flowers for another day and meeting with his many friends in downtown Lincoln Park in front of his five and dime store. This gentle little man will always live in my memories....

XX

A WARM SUMMER DAY IN 1940 AND A CREEK FULL OF RAIN WATER

A warm summer day in 1940 and a creek full of rain water, with the thought of our old wooden door that was our raft, and the frogs jumping, was all we three eight year olds needed to plan a hike to our favorite creek, next to the railroad tracks and Champaign Street. The creek we spent many a full summer day at, but now with it water filled meant floating about with the water usually over our ankles, due to our size, and watching the frogs, which meant good hunting. The sound of Eric and Bert calling my name under my window at 8:00 am, was good to hear, with my pockets full of wooden kitchen matches, a can of Campbell's vegetable soup, and four or five of my mother's day old cold potato pancakes safely wrapped in wax paper, plus the thought of feasting on wild raspberries that grew along the creek. So wearing our leather high tops and armed with my Daisy BB gun, the hike had started, with a two block walk to our creek.... Walking through ankle deep water in the flooded field in hopes of spotting a few snakes that would be doomed if I got a shot, I did and they were free for us to hunt another day. The railroad had a track crew that repaired the track bed, riding in the little rail carts loaded with tools, and they always waved as they passed us on the creek. An almost full day of eating berries, staining our faces, and catching five or six good size frogs that we put in a wooden Fargo pop case....wow....a real catch of the day! A track crew working nearby stopped and asked if we would trade our frogs for a ride on the work train. Would we! A dream come true. Helping us three kids onto the little train, wide eyed and hearts pounding, the work carts began to move faster and faster toward Detroit, passing Southfield and then Outer Drive and still moving, where the foremen watching our smiles turning to fear, stopped the little train North of Outer drive. We were thinking that it would stop and reverse, taking us back. Instead, we stood on the rail bed and watched the little train start up and disappear from view into Detroit, taking with them our Faygo pop case with the traded "catch of the day" and my can of vegetable soup. We slowly walked back to the safe haven of our creek, munching on my mother's cold potato pancakes which never tasted better to three eight year olds with berry stained faces ending our first adventure that far from home, to the safety of our wooden door raft and our creek still jumping with frogs.

XXI

WALKER SIGN COMPANY, FIREMAN ON TRUCKS AND DUNCAN YO-YO'S

Watching men from the Walker Sign Company using long brushes to paste strips of colorful advertising on the local bill-boards piece by piece about the city, to me was amazing to watch and a lost art for sure. Firemen riding outside on the rear of a fire engine, putting on their rubber coats, or fighting grass fires in the vast open fields using brooms and shovels, while dense smoke from the fires covering many neighborhoods.

Following a fire engine on your bike to a wailing siren, or watching them pitching horseshoes across from the fire station, then running to leave when a fire call came in. The 1940's also brought the Duncan Yo-Yo to life. I recall leaving class at Goodell School to see these young Yo-Yo masters performing in front of the school for us ten year olds...."walking the dog" or "rocking the baby". What magic to a little kid to witness, running home and out of breath, telling my mother what magic I had seen, and may I buy one from the savings in my toy bank. Like most mothers listening her almost out of breath son, she opened her purse and gave me small change to buy my Yo-Yo. Tried as hard as I could, I just could not get the "dog to walk" or the "baby to rock". It all looked so simple in front of the Goodell school only hours before, so the Yo-Yo was put in the dresser drawer where I would attempt to master this little piece of magic on a string another day.

XXII

MY FIRST SIGHT OF TELEVISON....

During the years of the 1940's, I remember approaching a small group of people standing in front of the "English Radio shop" at Fort Street and Garfield, staring at the front display window. Stopping and standing on my toes, I could barely see the small box in the window showing moving pictures. Pushing towards the front for a better view, seen a sign reading "Philco Televison" Wow!! The moving pictures with sound then changed to a wrestling show, bringing laughter from the onlookers. I was in total awe watching and listening to something that would change our lives in so many ways. Running home to tell my parents what I had just seen, and thinking of tomorrow evening, hoping to leave early with my mom and dad to be sure of getting a good close place in front of the display window, already showing a real live wrestling show, and staying until darkness, walking home talking of what we had just seen, and thinking that perhaps someday we could too have a television box in our house. And to think that the viewing at the little radio shop was all for free!

XXIII

THE GREAT
SNAKE HUNT

Heavy rains during the warm summer days, meant that one of our favorite hunting grounds would be under a foot of water, and the Garter snakes would be out in full force where the high school now stands. In the early 1940's it was a low grassy field that held rain water for days. Time to get our bows and arrows ready for the hunt.... My friend Eric and I both 8 years old, were the hunters because Eric's little brother Bert was just 6, and only had a little bow as his mother would not let him have arrows like his brother Eric until he was older. Their mother would not let Eric go anywhere without taking little Bert with him, so he was always with us "big guys". Bert was always happy to tag along even if he only had a bow minus the arrows.... Taking off our leather high tops and long stockings, pulling our knickers up over our knees and barefoot, it was time for the big hunt. Storing our high tops under the bleachers at the football field, we were on our way, walking through the warm rain water in our bare feet, with our bows at the ready for the kill.... The little snakes were plentiful but had nothing to fear from us young hunters. After a few wild shots with the arrows, the snakes were safe for us to hunt another day…. Back to the bleachers where we put our high tops back on and walked down Champaign Street toward our creek and the railroad tracks, stopping to pick a couple of ripe tomatoes from Mr. Aber's garden…..

XXIV

THE BEAUTIFUL BLACK MONSTER...THE 5:30PM RED ARROW...

Our favorite thing was waiting for the South bound, 5:30 pm, Red Arrow steam passenger train to roar through Lincoln Park as it did every other day. The faint sound of the train whistle while still in Detroit, heading our way began our young hearts pounding with excitement, so placing a penny on the rail, we stood well back on the gravel just as the beautiful black monster came into our view, smoke belching from the engine and whistle blowing as it now got closer to the Garfield Street crossing, the ground shaking and the engine rocking back and forth with steam and fire now visible in the engines fire box, the whistle now screaming as it approached Champaign, the three of us little guys huddled together with our hands over our ears as the Black Monster roared past us kicking gravel in all directions. As always the engineer leaning from his side open cab wearing his red bandana and goggles, never failed to wave at his little wide eyed audience below with wide open mouths as he passed.....

51

After the last passenger car passed with a few waves to us from the lucky people inside on a real train ride, the beautiful Black Monster suddenly becoming smaller and smaller until it was only little dot in the distance, but still hearing the faint steam whistle as it passed crossing after crossing in other little towns as it did here in Lincoln Park, I often wondered how many times the friendly engineer passed a bunch of little wide eyed little boys our age as he did at the Champaign crossing in Lincoln Park on his way South. Most little boys during the days of the steam trains, dreamed of one day becoming a steam train engineer on those big beautiful Black Monsters, as I did. The Black Monster always had a way of making our penny disappear from the rail, as we never found one again....but the experience of little boys being able to watch this thrill every afternoon at 5:30 pm was worth every penny lost....

XXV

MONDAYS SEEMED
TO BE LAUNDRY DAY

For reasons unknown, Mondays seemed to be laundry day for most of our neighborhood during the summers. The twin clothes poles in the back yards that held the rope clothes lines and on any given Monday I recall mothers carrying the heavy wicker baskets of fresh washed family clothing from the basement into the back yard for hanging. In those days most houses with basements had the double wash tubs and the old Maytag Wringer washing machine, meaning all the washed clothing had to be put through the wringer before being carried outside. Some homes still had the knuckle busting wash boards, we had one but it was seldom used.... Can still picture my mother in her cotton house dress and ever present apron, walking back and forth under the lines with a rag making sure they were clean before hanging....wooden clothes pins hung in a cloth bag on the pole. Hanging the large bed sheets meant keeping a couple of clothes pins in her mouth while putting up the sheets. The only dryers in those days was the warm sun and gentle breezes. Almost everywhere you looked in the neighborhood, the sights of white only bed sheets appeared like sails on old sailing ships.... A common sight was the old frayed towels and linens that were part of most family's hanging wash, mostly due to the hard days of the ongoing depression. During the cold winter months, most of the large sheets were hung in the basement or attic for drying, but many clothing items were still hung outside no matter how cold the weather. The sight of men's white long johns and overalls slapping together in the wind was not to be forgotten....To this day I am still in awe of hard working women of those had depression days, the lack of money, many families without jobs and a family to raise, they were a special breed no doubt! Now after years of suffering from the Great Depression, the coming of World War II meant even more new and unheard of suffering for even more long years to come….as I stated, a very special breed indeed!

XXVI

THE "SPOOKY HOUSE"

The spooky little house sitting on the back of the lot on Fort Park Street near the fire station, during the early 1940's, recalling now when my mother and I would walk past, she would tell me the story that the little house belonged to a Gypsy fortune teller, and that people would go to this house and pay to have their fortunes told, in hopes of hearing good news for them in the hard days of the depression years in Lincoln Park. I remember when selling the Saturday Evening Post magazine door to door, I decided to slowly walk to the front door of this little house without a porch in hopes of selling a Post. After a short time of not getting an answer I walked away. Telling my mother that I knocked on the door of the fortune teller's little house on Fort Park, she began telling me stories of traveling Gypsies who were mostly fortune tellers, who would kidnap children who were never seen again. As a little boy my young imagination went wild, that I was so close to a Gypsy's house knocking on the front door and then getting home safely.... So, after telling my friends my mother's story, we would cross the street well before this little spooky house, always looking over our shoulder as we hurriedly passed. Gone now is this little house with only a small patch of dirt still visible as a reminder of days past. Even now, when I have occasion to drive on Fort Park, I can't help myself not looking over and remembering the story from my mother about the traveling Gypsies and fortune tellers that were only a few short blocks from our house.

XXVII

DECEMBER 7, 1941

The war years, December 7, 1941 in Lincoln Park.... Japanese war planes have attacked our naval fleet early this morning on the island of Hawaii at Pearl Harbor causing deaths to thousands of military personal, STAY TUNED.... This broadcast came over our small radio Sunday evening December 7, 1941. This news flash interrupted the regular program, causing instant silence between by parents, then my mother began to cry loudly, I never witnessed my mother cry like this before, causing me to wonder, what is attacking the fleet and what is Pearl Harbor, but I realized it must something really bad for my mother to cry like this. My father appeared stunned, only saying we would be all right, in hopes of comforting my mother. As only nine years old I could not understand the meaning of war, or how it would affect us. Would the war planes come to Lincoln Park and when, and would we be killed when they did? Nothing was taught to us kids at Goodell School about the meaning of war, but I did not want to cry like my mother. Both parents lived through the First World War and knew the horrors of it, and now another war. Now looking back over the early years thinking how this changed Lincoln Park from a small quite town, to a place gearing for world war, Pearl Harbor changed Lincoln Park forever! Living without a telephone as did most of our neighbors, except a lone home telephone on Champaign Street, our small radio was the only news we had at the time. Neighbors began gathering in the street, woman openly crying and men just talking together, and I recall little kids continuing to play as darkness came. December 8, 1941, President Roosevelt came on the radio and spoke to the nation about this day of infamy, while Detroit's newspapers finally hit the streets, giving the people some news of what was to come…. Soon air raid drills would begin in Lincoln Park; this only bringing more fear to us. Each neighborhood was assigned a warden from the area, he being armed with an army helmet, gas mask attached to his belt, flashlight and whistle. As darkness fell on the hour of the air raid drill, it meant that all window shades had to be drawn and all lights out in the homes, leaving what seemed like hours, sitting in the dark but still listening to our radio for any news. The sound of the warden's whistle meant the all clear and the lights began to go on again in the city. With this, some of the fear left me as the bombers did not come that night, but what of tomorrow and the day after? Was this the end of the "sounds of silence" that I knew in my small world of Lincoln Park?

XXVIII

Slow Moving Trains Carrying The Machines of War.....

During the early days of World War II, we young boys continued to hunt daily with our BB guns, almost living at the creek during the warm days of summer. To seven or eight year olds, the new war was something very far away, and we really did not understand the true reality of it all. As we listened to the stories of our parents telling of the hard days of the World War I that they lived through. Suddenly, we kids began to see things that we had never seen or heard before, the flights of huge planes overhead and the neighborhood air raid drills. My Dad's little table radio on continually for any news of the world at war or the headlines in the daily newspaper of the horror of what was to come. But for us kids, the times of innocents, climbing trees, swimming in the muddy creek or just sitting in our underground bunk, began to change for us. Now instead of the joy of waiting for the speeding 5:30 Red Arrow steam train to pass, the railroad became a very different place for us. The endless slow moving freight trains drew out attention by showing us a different railroad that we knew from yesterday, now we would sit and wait for hours to witness the slow moving freight trains pulling flat cars with things that we had only seen in the Saturday news reels at the movies. Now there were live Army soldiers with guns riding on each passing flat car, guarding the tanks, trucks and artillery pieces coming out of Detroit's factories. It now seemed even more important to carry our BB guns in support of the soldiers that slowly passed us daily at the Garfield Street, crossing in Lincoln Park, giving them each a wave or hand salute as they passed slowly by. But the real thrill was when a real army soldier would smile and return the greeting with his salute. Little did we kids know that many of these same soldiers would be going to war shortly after passing through Lincoln Park on a slow moving steam train guarding the tools of war that would stay in our memories for some 70 years to come.

XXIX

Daisy BB Guns...The War Years

During the early years of WW II, we young boys continued our daily hunting with our Daisy BB guns, spending the warm days at our creek next to the railroad, roasting potatoes and eating wild raspberries in the area that now is I-75 and Champaign.... Our past days of stillness and almost silence, now ended, as the almost around the clock movement of freight trains coming from Detroit with endless flat cars carrying tanks, trucks, artillery pieces etc., bringing daily excitement to us kids, who had never seen anything like this except in the movies.... Each flat car carried an armed soldier, and as the slow trains lumbered along, almost every soldier was given a wave and a yell from the young dirty faced hunters, also armed with our Daisy's. Most soldiers returned our greeting with a military salute, "memories not soon forgotten"....

XXX

BOMBERS IN THE SKY

The usually quiet skies in the early years that we kids remembered from our sounds of silence days, now have been transformed almost overnight to a now busy highway in the skies of Lincoln Park, with the new Willow Run bomber plant turning out a B-24 heavy bomber, one every hour 24 hours, we now witness these same war planes on a daily basis flying over the city, sometime in small formations of five or six, to single flights...wow! To us kids it was something to see, but the real excitement for us was when a formation of P-38 fighter planes streaked overhead at high speeds, unlike the slow lumbering B-24s. I recall how we would wave our arms and cheer at the sight of these beautiful war birds, telling each they were on their way to bomb the "Japs", "like we really knew", but I guess they eventuality did.... At this time in the war years, the movies filled the screen of the Lincoln Park theater with our heroes and John Wayne with his goggles over eyes, diving his P-38 fighter into a Japanese formation of Zero fighters, and shooting them out of the sky as the theater erupted into loud cheers by the kids who paid their twelve cents admission weekly to watch with pride this spectacle. Not forgetting three cowboy movies and a half dozen cartoon pictures, John Wayne always lived to fight again next week as a pilot or a marine on Wake island, such an "American Hero" to the paying cheering audience of rowdy little Lincoln Park boys and girls. How great to be an American kid during these times, but little did we know the true horrors of war until years later!

XXXI

MY MOTHER BECOMES "ROSIE THE RIVETER"...

The theme "Rosie the Riveter" became associated with the thousands of woman who labored daily on our aircraft plants. Willow Run became the Bomber plant which also employed hundreds of downriver women. Many of our Lincoln Park mothers left their families for long periods of the day to share in the legacy of becoming "Rosie the Riveter". Beginning wages of ninety five cents an hour was attractive at the time, due to the many years of the depression, which finally ended with the war. It would be safe to say that the majority of the "Rosie's" had never held a full time job prior to this time. My mother and three other Lincoln Park women, traveled the long distance daily in an old car "with a bad heater" (in my mother's words), they worked long hours, six days a week, climbing in and out of these giant war planes, producing many a black and blue marks on their bodies.... Ford built the bomber plant which produced the B-24 four engine heavy bomber, the first in October of 1942, then turning out a single B-24 plane every hour around the clock, seven days a week, and at the wars end, a total of eight thousand six hundred B-24 heavy bombers for the war effort. I still find this unbelievable even to this day! At war's end, the plant ended the production of aircraft, and most mothers returned back home to their families, having lost precious years watching their children grow. In my opinion, these thousands of Americans and hundreds of downriver women have earned the title of being part of the **"GREATEST GENERATION"** in our history as **"Rosie the Riveter"**.

XXXII

WAR TIME RATIONING COMES TO LINCOLN PARK

War time rationing came to Lincoln Park during the early days of the war and consisted of almost everything used in our daily living....this had never been experienced by Lincoln Parkers before. Gas rationing meant that A-B-C- window stickers for only enough gas for work or business. All car production ended for the duration, while plants converted to war material. Food rationing, meat, butter etc. meant a ration book must be presented to the grocery for any purchase. Horse meat began to show up in butcher shops and finally in our home (as I learned years later) where my mother admitted that was the only meat choice for the family. My dad would drive to Windsor, Canada where there was no rationing, and hide his meat purchase in our 1937 Plymouth before crossing the bridge back into the USA…. At night, for fear of gas and tire theft, cars were parked inside locked garages, some remained on blocks for the entire war…. Families were asked to donate spare pots and pans (my mother took this hard) but she cleaned out the kitchen cabinets of items that she bought years earlier with saved small change. Bacon and cooking grease was saved and taken to the local butcher shop where it was later used in the making of ammunition for the war effort.... We kids would pull our wagons going door to door collecting waste paper, rubber, tin cans and any type of metal that was needed in the war. I remember my mother giving me a dime every Friday to take to Goodell School where it bought a war stamp which was placed in my stamp book, and years later turned into a war bond where years later it was valued at $18.75. All this instilled a real sense of pride in us young Lincoln Parkers.

XXXIII

Unpatriotic Not To Pick Up Navy Men Hitchhiking

Ford Motor in Dearborn had a small navy base on their property at the Rouge River at Schaefer Highway. My parents almost never failed to drive down Schaefer from Dix Avenue on weekends to shop at the Montgomery Ward store on Michigan & Schaefer in Dearborn. I remember that on weekends, the sailors were free to leave the base to visit Dearborn or other places. Schaefer Highway was filled with groups of sailors standing along the curb lane with their thumbs out looking for rides. My dad driving his 1937 Plymouth 2 door, would never ever fail to stop and pickup sailors headed for Dearborn, eager for the lift. As many as 4 would climb into the back seat with me at times sitting on the lap of a young navy man, until we reached Michigan Avenue and they would all pile out and go on their way.... My dad coming to this country in 1913 from Lithuania felt it would be unpatriotic for any one NOT to stop and give these men a ride whenever possible. Thinking back, I may have picked up the hitch hiking idea while proudly sitting on the lap of a young sailor in the back seat of that old 37 Plymouth. It was the right thing to do! Also, the naval air station on Grosse Ile, filled Jefferson Avenue from Trenton to Wyandotte, again by navy guys looking for a good time. I recall Biddell Avenue sidewalks with scores of walking military men and women. My sister 18 years old during this time told me that she and her girlfriends could not wait until the weekends to go to Bishop Park in Wyandotte to meet some of these young guys their own age and just dance and have a good time.

XXXIV

SACRIFICE...DURING
DARK DAYS
OF DEPRESSION
AND WWII...

When the history of Lincoln Park is written, it must include the many sacrifices made by all the hard working people of Lincoln Park, during the dark days of the depression years and those of World War II, over some 70 years ago....the term the "greatest generation" in which our military fought and died deserved this honor as their own, but in part to also include our parents and grandparents, who while still suffering the effects of the great depression, took part in the greatest war mobilization effort in our countries history. Auto plants and steel mills were transformed overnight to full production. Lincoln Parkers flooded the plants on a round the clock effort to produce what was needed by our military.... Single women, mothers and grandmothers made the daily two hour round trip by carpooling to the Willow Run bomber plant in Ypsilanti. Yesterday's stay at home mothers and grandmothers were suddenly climbing through giant B-24 super bombers, turning out one every hour, and at wars end, they produced 8600 B-24 for our air forces. My mother was included in this work force.... Lincoln Park's bus company suddenly added dozens of buses to carry out Lincoln Parkers to the round the clock shifts at the Ford Rouge, General motors and Chrysler plants around the Detroit area, as well as the Ecorse steel mills were geared for the massive war production. As a little boy I recall the buses returning to Lincoln Park, filled with tired and dirty workers, many falling asleep where they were seated, while many stood for the ride back for lack of seats, getting off at their stops, walking to their neighborhoods and homes, some blocks away, most with the ever present black lunch pail in their hands.... Most war production ran seven day a week with long hours on their respective shifts, families went days without seeing their father or mother, and in some cases both. Our city grew over night from a quiet little town, to a busy city with hundreds and hundreds of people coming from all over the country to the downriver area in the hope of jobs. Homes were built, schools were constructed and businesses opened to the thousands of transplants, most remained in Lincoln Park at wars end, discovering a fine place to raise a family and begin a new life.... From depression years to war years, our parents and grandparents became part of our new country, doing what was expected of them and of their families. Our tough Lincoln Parkers withstood fear and agony during these trying years, but built a fine city for their families and for their efforts to be part of the greatest generation is a term that fits our hard working families alike. We may never see another group of patriots as those who worked and built a fine city, while helping to win the most horrible war of their time. If the time ever comes again when people must come together, I am sure that the new breed of Lincoln Parkers will surly take up from their grandparents, and carry the heavy load as in the past. The term "the greatest generation" certainly "must" include these strong people known as Lincoln Parkers..

XXXV

CHILDREN OF THE GREATEST GENERATION 1941-45

Children of the greatest generation (1941-1945), were called upon to assist in the war effort by collecting everything from old newspapers, any type of scrap metal, old rubber tires and even bacon grease that was later used to make ammunition. I remember using my dad's old homemade wheelbarrow with the front spoked steel wheel, to go door to door with my friend Richard. Once it was filled, we pushed it to the collection area a couple of blocks away. We were a sight with our dirty hands and faces from the news print, only to go back to your neighborhood to refill and old wheelbarrow for another to unload.... A found old tire was a real prize as was bacon grease that mothers would place in Mason jars for collection. These efforts gave us kids a real sense of pride. Rationing of almost everything took over, tires, gas, most all meats, clothing and shoes.... I think we were allowed two pair of leather shoes a year. All car production ended, and in their place there were tanks, trucks and jeeps. You were allowed small amounts of gas, depending on the location of your job....car tires lasted for years. Many people locked their cars in their garages out of fear that gas and tires would be stolen....some family cars were put on blocks in the garage until the war ended. Homes were asked to donate any type of metal pot and pan that could be used for the war effort. My mother was near tears when she gave up her favorite cookware a couple of items, but to these people, this was fine and then pride took over.

XXXVI

DARK AND GOLD STARS IN THE WINDOWS

As the war continued, the sight of small banners hanging in the front windows of homes, banners with "Dark Stars", meant that someone from that home was away in the service. Then more and more "Gold Stars" began to appear, meaning a son or father was killed in action. Two "Gold Stars" was for families that lost more than one member. Walking past these "Gold Star" homes for a ten year old boy, I always felt a sense of sadness knowing that a grieving mother or wife was inside and how their life was changed forever.

XXXVII

THE "BARE ASS BEACH"
AND THE 5:30
PENN RED ARROW

Hot summer days during the early 1940's, was a time to head to our favorite swimming hole, the "B.A.B". With a pocket full of BBs for our Daisy BB guns and a mason jar of cold water, we three 8 and 9 year old kids began our long walk south on the railroad tracks from Champaign Street. Crossing London Street, there was a little house across the field that always had a couple of barking dogs running back and forth along the wire fence, so with our eyes darting towards the dogs, we began to walk a bit faster until we passed in safety. By now our mason jar of water was now half empty, and we had only walked a short distance, so the rest of the water was to be saved for the long walk back. In the distance we saw a bright light that we knew was on an incoming train going north. It became closer and we saw that it was a slow moving freight train, in passing, the engineer gave his us his usual friendly wave, and we walked on as the air was now filled with silence with the passing of the train now almost out of sight. Finally the railroad trestle was in sight, meaning our swimming hole was near as well. The muddy swimming hole was almost full due to the recent heavy rains. Stripping out of our clothes, we three jumped into the muddy warm water and looked up at the railroad trestle high above our heads. We knew that the 5:30 steam passenger train "The Penn Red Arrow" would be passing soon in the late afternoon as it always did, even from the past times of swimming here, we would go home after the train passed today. In the distance the sound of the steam whistle was faintly heard, meaning it was headed our way quickly. Now the whistle was heard at the London Street crossing, so it would pass over head on the trestle any second now, and with a roar kicking up gravel from the road bed, it passed over us naked kids in the muddy water, jumping up and down in full view of the passengers looking out the windows at the naked little boys. Wonder how many of the people were surprised at the sight they had just witnessed in the muddy waters below the trestle on their way South on the Penn Red arrow passenger train. Time for the long walk home and supper, putting on our clothing over wet bodies, we began the walk back laughing as we walked, talking of what we had just did…. three little Lincoln Park rowdies on their way to growing up. Our swimming hole was known by us as B.A.B. or "Bare Ass Beach" at which I still smile at today thinking about the fun days we kids had in the muddy water and the 5:30 Red Arrow steam train passing over head with a few shocked passengers aboard…

XXXVIII

WW II, Warm Summer Evenings and Band Concerts by Mr. Finley

Warm summer evenings during the years of World War II always meant a free band concert provided by the Lincoln Park high School Band and conducted by Mr. Finley with his baton in hand at the old wooden band stage on Fort Street just South of Southfield Road. As I recall, the concert was always a special treat for war weary Lincoln Parkers, who would carry their old wooden kitchen chairs and usually a blanket to be spread on the grass for the kids. Most families came with their suppers of fried chicken to be passed around. My dad never forgot his Thermos bottle of hot coffee and a large bottle of Sweet Sixteen pop for the kids. The concert always began with the band playing the National Anthem to a hushed crown standing with men holding their hats over their hearts. After a couple of songs, you would always see a couple dancing on the sidewalk to a popular song performed by the high school band. The sound of music on a quiet evening could be heard for blocks around and brought passing cars to stop and enjoy the music, and become part of Mr. Finley's audience. The sight of the ever present White Good Humor truck parked at the curb meant we kids could expect a dime for an Eskimo Pie ice cream sandwich, where your dad would usually get the first bite, hopefully a small one. Can still picture some of the mothers in their kitchen aprons, passing the evening supper to the hungry kids kneeling on the blankets. Mom would usually carry her little black small change purse in her apron's pocket, in the event another dime or two would be needed for another Good Humor desert. Good music and fun times for the families during those warm summer evenings seated in front of the wooden band stage and Mr. Finley always in band uniform with his baton during the hard days of World War II....

XXXIX

TRAVELING CARNIVAL'S AND SIDE SHOWS...

To a couple of ten year old Lincoln Park kids, the excitement began with the cardboard sign at Fort & Southfield announcing the coming Carnival and side shows. The warm summer days during the early 1940's, when the big trucks began parking in the field behind Fort Street and Southfield all the way to Electric Street always brought out most kids in the city as well as curious parents watching the unloading and setting up of the fun rides which seemed like they did it overnight. Most of us kids had never seen most of the modern kind of rides that were being constructed by the crews, but the one that caught my attention immediately was the "Loop O Plane"....Two little open air cockpits that went over and upside down as they passed each other in motion.... Paying my dime, I recall being strapped into the cockpit alone while my buddies stood back in envy due to their lack of a couple of dimes. The ride began, back and forth, over and over until it finally made a complete loop leaving me standing on my head many feet over the ground. After the first loop I realized that this was a mistake and wanted it stopped, but this was not to be. Loop after loop that seemed like forever, it seemed that my stomach was in my throat, and it was, as I then with a loud yell I began to vomit up the greasy hot dog I had a few minutes earlier, a couple of more loops and the operator finally realized he had a mess to clean up in that little tiny cockpit. After stopping the ride I staggered out in view of my laughing friends as well as many strangers…. From that day forward, the sight of kids waiting in line to get on this Loop O Plane, only made me shudder for them. All this for only a dime, but losing that greasy hot dog while in flight, caused me to walk home almost alone with my two buddies well behind me still laughing not wanting to get too close until I got home and changed out of those rotten knickers and long socks….

XL

SPRING CLEANING AND THE FRAYED LIVING ROOM RUG

I remember my mother stretching her lace curtains after washing, on a large wood frame with points all around the wood frame, where you would make sure the curtain was tight and not wrinkled. Every spring required spring cleaning throughout the old house. My mother would roll up the living room rug and carry it to the rear clothes line, place it over the line and proceed to beat the hell out of that poor old frayed dirty carpet with a carpet beater, looking something like a tennis racket, only bigger and made of metal. We didn't have an electric vacuum cleaner in those days, so mom would grab anyone of us (usually me) and I would begin the assault on that old carpet, where a cloud of dust would appear around your head as long as you beat that tired old carpet, which in places was so thin that you could see through it. As the only son in the house, it got to where I hated to see spring arrive in Lincoln Park, when my mother would announce spring cleaning time, she would say "son, help me roll up this carpet and carry it to the clothes line, it really needs extra cleaning this year". So here we go again, the assault on that poor old frayed living room carpet was about to begin and I needed a bath after it was over....

XLI

JACK TAYLOR ...CITY SANTA AND ONE MAN RECREATION DEPARTMENT

Remembering the Santa house during the early to mid-forties at Fort & Southfield as a kid of 10 years old, and the city Santa was always a Recreation Department worker by the name of Jack Taylor who fit the image of Santa to us kids due to his large mid-section, and his fake beard stained by his constant chewing of tobacco. We kids knew him better as Jack and not Santa, but we would always stand in line in the little unheated house hoping that somehow Jack would bring us something for Christmas.... Jack Taylor was a one man Recreation Department and as I recall, he would umpire school baseball games. He would put down the white lime lines on the football field, then work the chains on the sidelines during the games but not before installing the six foot canvas panels that encircled the entire football field in the afternoon of the game. I remember people bringing small ladders or standing on a box looking over the top of the canvas to avoid an admission fee of 50 cents.... When the game ended, Jack Taylor would begin the job of taking down the panels from the overhead wire and with the help of us little kids, fold up the canvas where it was put in the bed of Jack's old black pickup. After receiving the quarter that was promised, I would walk home across the dark open field to my house where my mother would be waiting, always inspecting my dirty pants and shirt which would be washed early the next morning. I with my quarter would hurry to Urban's little store for a Faygo cream soda pop and a Clark bar, nothing better as I now remember.... So another Christmas coming soon and we kids would line up early, thinking maybe there would be a real Santa and not a guy named Jack with the tobacco stained beard, but it seemed that Santa Jack would be waiting for us kids in the little unheated building as he was the year before. We never missed standing in the cold Lincoln Park winter hoping just maybe a real Santa would be inside....

XLII

RAILSPLITTER FOOTBALL, PEP RALLIES AND SNAKE DANCES

Living across the open field from LPHS, was a thrilling time for an 11 year old kid.... I recall the Railsplitter marching band rehearsing on the football field, days before the big game with Melvindale. The sound of the band could be heard for blocks around the empty fields of the neighborhoods of Lincoln Park, playing the Railsplitter fight song, "Lincoln Park High...Lincoln Park High...hail to orange and blue" to the music of the college fight song "On Wisconsin". The music would send chills down my back, and while walking back to Goodell school after lunch, the sounds could still heard as I entered the school, a couple of blocks away.... I recall as a kid, the night before a game, students building a large wood pile at the rear of the school, which would be burned as part of the Pep Rally with teachers and students alike singing and dancing while the fire burned.... On game day, Fridays saw a large number of students running from the school to form what was called as a "Snake Dance". With the band music playing, the dance consisted of students forming a single line of boy-girl-boy-girl holding onto the waist of the person in front of them, then "snaking" across Champaign Street and back to the football field, all during the dance, more and more students would join in singing the fight song of the Railsplitter, just laughing and having a good time. To this kid, the Pep Rallies were more fun to watch then the game itself. I would run alongside of the "snake dance" to watch wide eyed as my older sister, now a senior, would join in at the front of the dance…. Leaving now, as the big game is about ready to kick off…. LET'S GO RAILSPLITTERS!!!!!!!

XLIII

THE MEMORIAL PARK CIRCUS AND ROAD SHOW...

Before the church and the Band shell were in place, the city would give permission to a number of traveling road shows and the circus to bring that type of entertainment to city property at Fort and London in the early 1940's. Colorful window signs began announcing the arrival of the road show and circus early and it seemed that most telephone poles also had signs nailed to them. It was an exciting time to a bunch of 10 year olds, who had never seen a circus or traveling road show before. Almost overnight, the park was filled with large tents of all types, and the large carnival rides of the day. The loud music over the loud-speakers announced that shows and rides were open for business, so we kids were almost the first ones to spend the entire day gawking at the colorful painted canvas which showed some of the many wonders of the world or "freaks" as they were called. Two headed cows, the world's thinnest man, the tallest lady, and the bearded lady were all in Lincoln Park to be seen in person.

Every tent, had a wooden stage in front before the entrance, which included a guy called the "Barker". With the loudspeakers blaring out music, the "Barker" would collect a crowd of mostly a male audience, by bringing out four or five scantily dressed ladies, slowly moving with the blaring loudspeaker music. The "Barker" would yell out to the group of gawkers that the show inside would began shortly, and for the price of a quarter, it was yours to see and enjoy. The male audience began to grow larger and larger as the ladies of all ages and sizes smiled down on them from the little stage. Wow! To us kids, who probably only had a quarter between us, this was exciting, but it was not to be, so anything free for us was okay. At another large tent and stage with blaring music, the "Barker" would yell out, for only one thin dime, who could see the two headed cow and the bearded lady inside. The show was about to begin….people were paying a dime to see something that would only be seen once in a lifetime. More large tents and stages had colorful painted canvases describing all what was offered inside for a dime. We kids were attracted to the stage of the magic show where the "Barker", who would bring out a fire eater, a pretty lady who would stick pins through her lips. We kids shuddered at this. Once the "Barker" looked down at me and asked me to come up on the stage and assist him in a magic act. I recall a man pushing me up on the stage, where I stood frozen with fright looking out at the crowd of people staring at me…. My first thoughts were, what my mother or dad would do if they knew that their little boy was on a stage in full view of our neighbors. The "Barker", holding a small tin bucket under my right ear, caused the "clunk" sound of a silver dollar falling in the bucket. I was now wide eyed and amazed! How could he pull a silver dollar from my ear? Then he did the same by putting the tin bucket under my nose, again, another silver dollar "clunked". Finally the stage act was about over, and after being half pushed off the stage by the "Barker" he yelled again out to the viewers, the show inside was about to begin, and for only a little dime…. Walking away, I was still in awe. How did this happen to me? He called it magic! The roar of a motorcycle speeding around a wooden wall was in the next tent…. I recall that people were flocking in to see this, but we kids were content to just hear the roar of the motorcycle, standing outside…. It was all to see in how "Memorial Park" after a couple of days the circus and the "Barkers" had disappeared overnight as quickly as they appeared a few days earlier. We kids were already planning next year when the circus would return. Next time we wanted to have a have a few "thin dimes" in our pockets in hopes of seeing the two headed cow in person.

XLIV

RAILSPLITTER FOOTBALL GAMES... MY JOB SETTING UP

Railsplitter football, 70 years ago....During the mid-forties, the LPHS football field would be completely encircled by sections of canvas, six feet tall and ten feet long all suspended by an overhead wire. A single front gate with a small admission booth would admit the hundreds of people and students for the game of the year. Both the Lincoln Park side and the visitors side had the old wooden bleachers, and during the height of the game with the fans jumping up and down in excitement, it was a miracle they didn't collapse. Any fan that was over six feet tall, could just stand outside the canvas wall and look over the top at the entire game....game ended, not sure who won! The LP recreation manager "Jack Taylor" would then enlist certain kids to assist in rolling up and loading the panels of canvas onto a large flat trailer for storage. This was a big deal to us kids who were promised the unheard wage of 50 cents for our labor. It was dirty and heavy work, but the thought of 50 cents made it worthwhile until

I got home at 11:00 pm, and my mother standing on the front porch awaiting her little boy, my clothing filthy from the loading of the canvas. Her remarks to me were loud and clear....never again! It was early up on Saturday morning and a bike ride to Jack Taylor's house on Philomene, to collect my wages from the night before. To this day, I could never understand a man answering his door so early in the morning with a mouth full of chewing tobacco, he was never without a mouth full of chew I remember. He gladly paid me the 50 cents, and this kid went riding with two quarters in his pocket to Chiarelli's market for his favorite Faygo cream soda, with still a pocket of coins for ice cream later, thinking, this working is not such a bad deal!

1947 Lincoln Park High School Freshman Basketball Team, I am 3rd from the right, 2nd row

XLV

BOBBY SOCKS, SADDLE SHOES AND THE LUNCH BELL..

Bobby socks and saddle shoes, early to mid-1940's with the ringing of the lunch bell at Lincoln Park High School, and the exodus of hundreds of students, many loading into the few student cars heading to their favorite lunch spot. The throngs walked down Champaign Street heading to Urban's little restaurant and confectionary on the corner of Fort Park & Champaign. I can still recall the aroma of hamburgers and hot dogs cooking on the grill, filling the small building, while the Wurlitzer juke box played records at full volume for five cents a song, to the sounds of Glenn Miller, Tommy Dorsey and other big bands of the era.... Remembering the pretty high school girls, dressed in school colored sweaters, plaid skirts, white bobby socks and black & white saddle shoes, dancing with school lettermen in their blue and orange school sweaters and brown loafers over white sweat socks. The late comers, not able to get inside the crowded building, were left standing out front on the sidewalk, some taking advantage of the loud music dancing while holding a bottle of Coke. Any one from that era will admit that Fort Park & Champaign during the forties was the place to dance, laugh and walk back to school hand in hand with your steady. Another lunch bell and the whole thing would begin again - dancing, laughing and holding hands and slowly walking back down Champaign to a yet another class at Lincoln Park High School. What GREAT memories of that time!

XLVI

FRIDAY NIGHTS AT THE ROLLER RINK

Memories of people and places….Friday nights in the mid 1940's at the LP Roller rink with school friends, your rented black men's shoe skates, cruising the floor to the recorded organ music, selected by owner Jim Seats and his ever famous announcement of "all skate" where the floor would be filled by early teen age boys trying to look cool as they skated past the pretty girls. I remember they seemed better skaters than the boys….some of us looking like the Three Stooges with our feet going in all directions trying not to fall in front of the girls, and the embarrassment when it finally would happen. Not looking "so cool" in front of the laughing girls, how humiliating to a twelve year old when your main interest was to show off your skating talents, of which I had none. Soon it was time to skate to the soda bar for a Coke and hoping the music would end so that you could be the first kid out the door ahead of the pretty girls, only perhaps to do it again next Friday night. I wonder if the gum board is still there?

XLVII

EDDIE CLEMENTE SR. AND LEONE REMEMBERED

I believe Eddie Sr. was the first born to the Clemente family.... I remember a quiet, friendly man of large stature, who was an ex-professional football player and wrestler who always had a warm greeting of "how you doing" to almost everyone. Eddie Sr. could always be identified by the black twisted Italian cigar in the corner of his mouth. I don't recall it ever being lit but it was always a part of him.... Back in 1940 or 41, we little kids playing on Champaign Street remember Eddie Sr. walking his small goat on a rope, and wearing a full length raccoon coat and a Porkpie hat, made popular by Buster Keaton in the silent movies "Hi Eddie". We would yell from across the street, and he would wave back to us little 8 or 9 year old kids. He would walk to the rear of the LPHS and then return back walking toward Fort Park and I guess his home. Funny how even the littlest of things will stay with a person for a lifetime....Eddie Sr. a quiet sole, R.I.P. from the little kids on Champaign Street some seventy years ago. Leone was the original owner of Shorty's Bar, first built in the early years. "Shorty" was Mr. Leone's nickname due to his height, and I knew his son "Ray Leone" for much of the early years. I believe the brick family home at the corner of Fort Park & Philomene, still stands. The only Leone son, Raymond, took over the operation from his dad after his death, and did rename it the Sidestreet…. Charlie Chiarelli the first owner of the market across the street and Mr. Leone came from the same village in Italy to LP together through Ellis Island.

Sitting on the hood of a 1936 Ford with my mother's 410 shotgun getting ready to go pheasant hunting, 1948

XLVIII

THE LOCAL BUS COMPANY...

The building on the S.E. corner of Southfield and Lafayette, was built around 1945 or 46, and was owned by the LP bus company, where they used to park and repair Lincoln Park buses. There was a large overhead door on the rear and the front that exited onto Southfield. I walked past this building daily on my way home from Lafayette school, during seventh and eighth grade. As I recall the buses ran as far South as Fort Street to Eureka, turning and running North through Wyandotte, through all of Lincoln Park and continuing to downtown Detroit. Monday through Friday, the bus stopped on Fort Street and every second block would be filled with Lincoln Parkers in the early morning hours on their way to work in downtown Detroit.... The buses also ran on Southfield to routes as far as Dearborn, Southfield to Dix, North on Dix to Schaefer and then on to Michigan Avenue and back again. I recall on hot summer days the buses filled with tired hot workers making the return trip from downtown Detroit, many standing for the return ride due to filled seats, windows wide open for a little hot air, (no air conditioning in those days). It seemed that most would get off at Southfield and Fort in order to board another bus making the Southfield route. Many were going shopping in the many stores and shops that filled downtown Lincoln Park, then making the long walk to their homes, only to do it all over again their next work day. My future wife was one of the people that transferred to the Southfield bus to get off at Washington Street or just walk home from Fort Street….

XLIX

THE GOOD HUMOR ICE CREAM MEN AND GREYHOUND BUSES

Good Humor ice cream trucks ringing the bells as it came down your street, and running as fast as you could to get a dime from mother before it passed by, but the driver dressed in all white with a black bow tie, would most always stop and wait if he saw you running for home, yelling, wait, wait, I'll get my money. All this for a ten cent sale to an out of breath little kid who ran back clinching a dime in his closed fist....later replaced by the kid riding the three wheel bike with the ice cream box on the front, still with the little row of bells on the handle bars. We didn't always have the patience to wait as did the Good Humor man did.... I remember that both had the silver money changer on their belt. This belongs in the Good Humor hall of fame for sure!

I also have memories of people standing with little suitcases and cardboard boxes, waiting for the Greyhound bus to stop at Fort & Arlington in front of the Rexall drug store, for their trips to all points south. The uniformed driver placing their belongings in the secure storage area under the bus, which had no restroom on board, sometimes praying for the first rest stop the driver would make, usually at a restaurant on your way south. Many passengers carried their lunch on board, and the smell of everything from fried chicken to sardines and crackers would fill the bus....the lucky ones got off at Toledo!

L

SETTING BOWLING PINS...A GREAT JOB FOR A KID IN 1940'S

The closing of the Fort Park Bowling Alley ended an era for me in Old Lincoln Park where as an early teen I spent many a weekend and night time hours setting pins in that great old smoke filled place. It offered many Lincoln Park teenagers jobs when we were too young to work elsewhere. You have to be almost middle to old age to remember when there were pin boys at the end of the alley and not automatic pinsetters.... Each night there were two leagues, one beginning at 7 pm and the second at 9 pm, so that work was over shortly after 11 pm, unless some of the bowlers decided to bowl extra games. We were paid five cents a game. I once calculated how many tons I lifted during the four hours, but can't remember the total now.... I do know that the ball weighed at least 15 pounds and each pin probably weighted four or five pounds. On some nights you were given the chance to "jump alleys" which meant you set pins on both alleys, meaning double pay for double work. I quickly learned how to pick up as many as six pins with one stoop and learned how to pick up the heavy ball with a flick of my wrist and send it back on the ball return, and quickly learned exactly how high I had to lift my feet so that the ball or pins wouldn't hit my legs. I remember after the league ended for the night, some of the bowlers would roll a quarter or a fifty cent piece down the alley for a job well done by the thirteen year kid. We were paid in cash every evening by Mrs. James, so walking home in the dark with a couple of bills and some change in your pocket was a great feeling. I would be thinking of the next night when Mrs. James, always with a cigarette in her mouth, would give me a wink standing at the counter, meaning I was on the payroll for the night with the older guys.... An era indeed ended for me!

LI

MUST BE A SPECIAL PLACE IN HEAVEN FOR THE DOOR TO DOOR SALESMAN

Remember when you could hold a cookware demonstration in your home for six or eight of your good friends, and the company selling the cookware, would come in and personally cook a complete dinner to demonstrate their pots and pans? If they took an order in your home, the home sponsor with get a free set. Or the Kirby or Hoover vacuum cleaner salesman, coming to your door, to demonstrate their vacuum cleaners? They would vacuum your living room or more if you requested....or what ever happened to the Fuller brush salesman, knocking on your door with his large demo case of almost every brush ever made inside. We would always buy something small to get him to leave and go next door after telling him that we were sure our neighbor really needed brushes, and they probably were at home now. What a tough way to earn a living by going door to door, and having doors slammed in your face all day every day and then meeting people like me! Or the little old man peddler with the huge suitcase that would walk Fort Street, going into every gas station and bar selling shoelaces, pencils and men's personal items. I remember this little guy doing this for years. I am sure there must be a special place in heaven for peddlers and door to door salesman.

LII

HAYRIDES AND TOBOGGAN PARTIES...

Mention the word "hay rides" to some of the younger generation of today, and you get a puzzled look, like more old time stories from him again. Well, here I go anyway! The first memory of being part of a real live hayride was back in 1947 or 48 that was being put on by the Lincoln Park high school cheerleaders. To be invited to a hayride from a team member was something to remember and later to brag about. I believe a total 14 kids would head out to Lucky stables in the outback of Taylor, mostly dirt roads where street lights were unheard of. The covered hay wagon was pulled by a farm tractor for a couple of hours of singing and laughing with the kids to the little portable radio, then back to the stable and the modern recreation room complete with juke box and the latest records. Afterward some of the parents would come to pick us up for the trip back to Lincoln Park. The cold winter days of early high school days always meant that a note would be brought to the school office door, and on a certain evening, usually a Friday, the cheerleaders would plan for a group of kids to go to Rouge Park for a Toboggan party. You were asked to "sign up now" if your family had a toboggan and you were asked to bring it. There never seemed to be a shortage of snow or cold in those days, if we were lucky, two or three cars were available to go. With a couple of Toboggans tied to the roofs, it was usually seven or eight to each car, most with bad heaters, when the singing would begin finally ending at the park. There was always screaming as toboggans raced down the icy covered runs at high speed....then the long walk back up the steps to the beginning and doing it all over again. After a couple of hours and cups of hot chocolate from the stand, it was time to head back, with more singing and laughing from the three car caravan until home again in Lincoln Park. My memory of these great times of over sixty years ago, to me, the word "corny" never came to our young minds, I guess we all were just "old fashioned".

LIII

THE RUMBLE SEAT & WOLF WHISTLE....

To own a car during the 1930's usually meant that the wonderful "Rumble Seat" was available on the smaller coupe models (i.e. a seat directly behind the driver and outside that opened into an "open air girl watcher"). Cruising Fort Street in my buddy's 1930 Ford coupe on a warm summer evening, just the two of us with the open but empty rear "Rumble Seat" was a great attraction to girls walking together. The driver could operate the "Wolf Whistle", something new in the mid 1940's, by pulling on a small wire that would send out a loud "whistle" type of greeting to anyone walking on the sidewalks. The startled girls would scream and then laugh and always a wave to the two guys passing them. A ride in the "Rumble Seat" on a warm summer evening was not to be turned down, especially when they were school friends. So with fifty cents worth of gas, it was safe to cruise as far away as Wyandotte. Inviting two girls from the neighborhood, we were head for a favorite ice cream shop and with our double dip cones, it would be time to drive back to Lincoln Park. My buddy would never turn down the chance to use the "Wolf Whistle" when passing a couple of girls, and always with the same reaction by them, a wave while laughing together. It never failed. But a dirty look was always in order from the girl seated next to you in the open air "Rumble Seat". Early air conditioning was provided by simply cranking the small front windshield open. It not only provided you with air but bugs as well, or an outside antenna to hang your wet bathing suits on returning from a day at the Twin Lakes in Monroe. To be really cool we added a foxtail to our antenna that we bought at the Western Auto Store.

LIV

Hitchhiking to Twin Lakes and the 1938 Funeral Hearse...

It was only natural that my old memories went back to the mid and late forties in Lincoln Park. The fact that backyard swimming pools were almost unheard of, we Lincoln Park teens had an almost daily dream of getting a ride to the beautiful "Twin Lakes" in Monroe county. Any teen lucky enough to have access to transportation for the day was the most popular around. We kids did at times hitch hike on Telegraph Road to Twin Lakes Road, but then it was still a four or five mile distance down this country road to the entrance of the old stone quarry known as Twin Lakes, and getting a ride down the old road was almost unheard of.... An old buddy a couple of years older than I, working in Detroit, for whatever reason, bought an old 1938 funeral hearse for almost nothing as I recall, so if you didn't mind riding in the back of an old hearse (still breathing) you were welcome to board the Telegraph Road express as we called the old Packard, but for a day at Twin Lakes anything was worth it. I recall Charlie would collect 50 cents from each passenger for gas, and off we four to seven kids would go. I can never forget the look on the face of the old farmer that collected the 50 cent fare as the long black hearse pulled up filled with kids for the first time. After that it was no big deal to him, as he got to know the Lincoln Park rowdies. I still recall the tower we jumped from into the ice cold quarry water, and the cement dance floor next to the juke box that never stopped playing. When it was time to head back, wet bathing suits were hung from the door handles and the express headed back to stop at Bob-Jos where the looks from the customers never ended. Then home, but the first time that Charlie came to my house and blew the horn for me, my poor mother almost fainted at the sight of the black hearse waiting for me. That ended that, now I was dropped off at the high school and crossed the field to my house. Charlie parked the hearse behind a gas station on Southfield, as his parents forbid the old Packard to be parking in front of their home. I think that it was the summer of 1947 or 48 was when Charlie was forced to sell the old Packard. It was back to hitchhiking on Telegraph Road to enjoy the day at the old quarry, but never forgetting the old black beauty filled with teens and truck inner tubes for a fun time I still remember today.

LV

THE LONG WALK BACK
TO LINCOLN PARK FROM
TRAVERSE CITY...

The long walk back to Lincoln Park.... During the summer of 1945, the term "stupid is what stupid does" was invented by three 13-14 year old Lincoln Park boys. The plan....to hitch hike a ride to Traverse city, in hopes of making a pocket full of money by picking cherries at harvest time, and then returning on a Greyhound bus back to Lincoln Park. After a week or so, from here it only gets worse, we three met at Southfield & the railroad in the early morning hours, all with our small bed rolls and little cardboard suitcases....this was years before I-75 was even dreamed of. Jack, our 14 year old leader, had our route planed with his dad's old gas station map. How many drivers would actually stop and pickup three young kids with bed rolls and suitcases? This never entered our young minds and so we intended to head north as planned. Surprisingly, a salesman did stop and almost welcomed his three young travelers for his trip. When he reached his destination, it was back to hitchhiking with dreams of making big money. We walked and rode to the outskirts of Traverse City passing cherry orchards mile after mile. First we had to find a place to sleep and then get a job in the morning. We came upon a row of empty railroad box cars with the doors open – perfect. A great place to sleep, the box car that we started to climb into was already occupied by migrant farm workers. They began to yell at us and stomp their feet, causing us kids to run wide eyed for our young lives, still clinching our bed rolls and little suitcases. When we ran out of breath, we stopped and a new vote was taken, it's back to Lincoln Park and safety. The problem now was that we had no money for the bus back home. We began walking on a dark highway without ever seeing a car, slept in a cornfield awaking wet from the morning dew, eating our saved peanut butter sandwiches still wrapped in wax paper. Tired and hungry, we got short rides but walked forever....finally a ride to Dearborn as darkness began. In 1945 Southfield was only a two lane divided road with little traffic after dark. We began our walk through Dearborn, Allen Park and finally, Lincoln Park which never looked so good, to three hungry, dirty and tired kids as we reached our houses. Our adventure brought a few laughs among us some years later, and I can't help but smile when driving into busy Traverse City today, wondering if they still leave railroad box cars with their doors open inviting night occupants to spend the night!

LVI

ALL THIS SERVICE FOR UNDER A BUCK...

The days of driving into a "service station" as they were called then, with only pocket change for gas was not unheard of. Crossing over the two rubber hoses in the drive way of the "service station" would instantly ring a little bell inside where two smiling attendants in clean uniforms and black bow ties, would hurry to service your car. Before you could order your fifty cents worth of gas, your front windshield was being cleaned and the attendant would be heading for the back window. The usual term by the attendant was "fill it up sir?" even though you were only 16 years old and you replied "fifty cents please" which bought you two a little over two gallons of gas in the 1940's. That never stopped the man from raising your hood and checking the oil, battery and water in the radiator....all this service for only under a buck! I'll never forget the early days at Deschaw & Moning Mobile station at Fort & Lincoln. Go inside and raise the lid on the pop cooler, always filled with ice, you could take your pick of any ice cold bottle of pop. Need a road map? They were free for the asking!

*November 1950, just turned 18 years old, in Kaesong, South Korea,
with my friend Jim Margolis, 5 months after the outbreak of The
Korean War, July 1950. My company was one of the first troops
brought in. One month later, December 4th, I would be airlifted out
of Pyongyang, North Korea due to severe cold injury at the Chosin
Reservoir / Campaign.*

*Memorial Day Parade 1963 with my son Donald Lee
Wallace. I was a member of the Police Marching Unit that led the
parades down Fort Street.*

LVII

Reminiscing of People and Things From My Youth...

I would be remiss or neglectful, if I didn't mention certain Lincoln Parkers from my growing years, and remember so vividly during the past seventy years of my life.

- "Max Paul"- principal of Goodell school during the 1940's, who took the time to teach a few little boys how to shoot a basket in the old school gym.
- "John Urban" – Urban's grocery, who gave me my first paying job at eight or nine years old, as the store delivery boy who had his own wagon for deliveries in the neighborhood.
- "Clyde Campeau" janitor at Goodell School in my young years, helping him and my friend carry out the school's furnace ashes to be spread about the playground earning us both fifty cents to share between us.
- "Charlie Chiarelli" – Chiarelli's grocery store, who helped my mother during the depression years in Lincoln Park.
- "Howard" - the friendly manager of the Lincoln

Park Show.

- "Gus" - Lincoln Park fruit market and "Mary" from the Lincoln Park Sweet Shop....always helpful to families during hard times of the 1930's.
- "Mr. Finley" - so may fond concert memories, from the old grey wooden band stage on Fort Street, always dressed in his band uniform and waving the baton, brought a lot of joy to us all.
- "Mickey Karol" – Karol's grocery, always a kind word to a little kid with only a nickel or dime to spend in his little store.
- "The double amputee" - selling pencils from his cloth cap in front of Neiser's Five and Dime.
- "Max" - the old black gentleman with a limp, who washed cars at the gas station at Fort & White Street. Everyone had a kind word for "Max".

Later year's memories:

- Buck and Hazel Anderson party store - helped so many neighbors during hard times, can't forget the pencil always on his ear.
- "Ernie and Billy Jean" – Carter's hamburgers, loved them both over the years, and Ernie's down home accent.
- "Howard the flower man" - none of us kids from the late 1930's ever knew his last name, but it didn't matter, the only word he ever used to us little kids and the business people in downtown Lincoln Park was "Hi"…. a very special person….

Just a few of the many fine people that remain in my memories for so many years, I could go on and on….

LVIII

COMING BACK HOME
AND REMINISCING...

Returning back to Lincoln Park and "home" during the summer of 2012....I usually do this a few times every year to spend a few weeks at our summer cottage in northern Michigan. I was determined to visit and walk the streets and old neighborhoods that were part of my young years beginning in 1937. Our old McLain house is still there and looking better than I ever remembered. I walked on McLain toward Fort Park, past the old wonderful house of Mrs. Cooper and her wonderful fresh baked bread. It brought a smile to my face and I hoped to recapture the aroma again. Next door is the little lot that once was the home of "Howard the flower man" who still lingers in my memory after some seventy five years. A short pause, then I regarded the old urban grocery at Champaign, which looked almost as I remembered. Goodell School has long gone to progress, but still the memories of ice skating on the small ice rink next to the school in my sister's white ice skates, or playing in the sandbox during the summer vacations while being supervised by Miss Betty who taught us games and crafts (later a principal at Carr school) still come to mind. I then passed by the old Martin family owned little hamburger place on Champaign where my mother and I enjoyed a hamburger and a pop under a large shade tree in 1937. My old Lincoln Park high school is gone and has been replaced by a new middle school….glad I was not there to witness that old wonderful building being taken down. My "bunk" is now gone too…. I crossed the street to view the new school football field and bleachers (which are very impressive), then stood in the high school parking lot looking through the wire fence at fast moving traffic on I-75, now on my creek and raspberry fields that I remember so well. Glancing at the railroad where we kids learned to love the old "Red Arrow" steam passenger train speeding south, still picturing the engineer in his red neck bandanna and goggles, waving as he passed. It was now time to turn and walk away from my memories with a lump in my throat and a tear in my eye, from the old wonderful times of floating in the creek on that old wooden door, now a fast moving freeway. Don't look back! Driving to the Lafayette school that I graduated from in 1947, with Mr. Gibson handing out the diplomas, always with that smile on his handsome face, it is now replaced by a modern building that reminds me of a box. I did not expect to see any major improvement on the North end of the city, but was very impressed with the "Fort Street Brewery" where we had lunch with new found friends from Facebook, good food, good service and an almost filled to capacity lunch crowd. In my heart I expected to see more development along Fort street, but with the "Fort Street Brewery" doing so well, this could be the spark that is needed to possibly make the difference in the future of the city. Lincoln Park and the Downriver are really no different from other small cities in the country, which all suffer from lack of funds and the economy. Did I expect a miracle when I returned? I guess in my heart I did, but not it was not to be….

LIX

IN CLOSING....LINCOLN PARK HISTORY...

When the history is written of Lincoln Park, it must include the many sacrifices made by the early to late days of World War II over some seventy years ago. The term the "Greatest Generation" in which our military fought and died around the world fully deserves this honor, and in part to also include our parents and grandparents, who are still suffering the effects of the great depression of the 1930's. Now with December 7, 1941, the effects would become even greater in dealing with a world war. Americans and Lincoln Parkers took part in the greatest war mobilization ever in our history. Detroit's auto plants and steel mills were transformed overnight for full war production. Lincoln Parkers flooded the plants around the clock to produce what was needed by our military. Kids going door to door, collecting waste paper and scrap metal in their little wagons, teens holding paper drives in high schools, and my 25 cent weekly allowance to buy a war stamp at Goodell School. Lincoln Park mothers and grandmothers began carpooling daily to make the two hour round trip to the Willow Run "Bomber plant" in Ypsilanti. Yesterday's stay at home moms, suddenly were climbing through the giant B-24 super bomber, turning out one bomber every hour, and 8,600 by the war's end in 1945. My mother was part of this work force. Lincoln Park Bus Company suddenly added dozens of extra buses to carry the hundreds and hundreds of Lincoln Parkers to the round the clock shifts at the Ford Rouge, General Motors and Chrysler plants in the Detroit area, as well as the increased production needed at Great Lakes steel in Ecorse. As a little boy, I remember the buses filled with dirty tired production workers, many falling asleep in their seats while many stood all the way home for the lack of seating on these mostly old bumpy buses, getting off at their corners, and walking the many blocks home for some, with their black empty lunch box swinging as they waked dead tired to their homes. The hot summer days kept all the bus windows wide open to provide fresh air, men seated next to the open windows, with their arm resting on the open window sills.

Most war production ran seven days a week with long hours. Some families went days without seeing either the mother or father, and in some cases both. Our little city grew almost overnight from a small quiet town, to a noisy busy city, with hundreds of transplant workers with their families coming from all over the country, to the downriver area to take part in the war effort. Homes, businesses and schools were built almost overnight to satisfy the needs of the people. New faces were seen daily in the little local stores, and traffic increased to flows never before seen in our small own. At war's end, thousands remained in Lincoln Park and the downriver area, discovering a fine place to begin a new life and family. From depression years to war years over night, our parents and grandparents became part of a new country, doing what was expected of them and their families. Our tough neighbors withstood fear and agony during these long war years, but in the end built a fine place for their children and grandchildren alike. Being part of the "Greatest

Generation of Americans" is a term that was earned by hard working people of Lincoln Park and the downriver area. We may never witness another group of patriots such as those who worked and built a fine city while helping to win the most horrible war of their time. But, if the time ever does come for them to come together again as they did in the 1940's, I am sure that the new breed of parents and grandparents will again carry the heavy load that their forefathers did so well before them.

Working on boyhood stories in my sunroom in Loudon, TN March 2013

Jean and myself at the Bald River Falls in East TN,
May 2011

ACKNOWLEDGEMENTS

This book is written in memory of my parents Julia and Walter Wallace. My father arrived in this country on his own in 1913 from his native county, Vilnius, Lithuania at the age of 18. He settled in Detroit in 1922, met and married my mother in 1927 and raised two children, my sister Norma and myself. He had a small two bedroom home framed out in 1937 in Lincoln Park and completed building much of the home himself. Hard working, law abiding Americans always. Missed but never forgotten.

My loving son Bruce, without his tireless efforts, this book would not have been possible. Special thanks go out to our friend and colleague, Jesse R. James who was the catalyst for the project along with Elizabeth Wallberg who completed the final edit and corrected all my grammar mistakes...yes she had her hands full. A extra special thanks go to all my Lincoln Park friends whom have read my stories on the internet and encouraged me to continue writing them and publishing them into this book.

I hope you all enjoy my stories which are as real and alive in my memory as they were the day they happened....

My son and co-author, Bruce and I, holding the
final draft (or at least we thought it was...) of my stories.

16590054R00080

Made in the USA
San Bernardino, CA
09 November 2014